BUSINESS IDEAS
TO MAKE A
MILLION DOLLARS
or Some
MONEY SOMETIME

JOYCE SHEARIN

Order this book online at www.trafford.com
or email orders@trafford.com

Most Trafford titles are also available at major online book retailers.

Print information available on the last page.

ISBN: 978-1-4907-9891-2 (sc)
ISBN: 978-1-4907-9893-6 (hc)
ISBN: 978-1-4907-9892-9 (e)

Library of Congress Control Number: 2019920844

Trafford rev. 12/20/2019

North America & international
toll-free: 1 888 232 4444 (USA & Canada)
fax: 812 355 4082

All Business Ideas To Start
(Please Obtain Needed Permission)

Business To Start:

- Weavelwigs made in America.

- Adjustable size ivory teeth sold over the counter for humans/people.

- Prescription contacts and prefilled eyeglasses. Prescriptions over the counter.

- Open a self service mobile vendor snack cart or self service.

- Liquid dental mouthwash.

- Open a karaoke internet café.

- Build premade small homes below current price.

- Start neighborhood bingo community casino.

- GED Book with Diploma in back - $50.00

- Digital Reader ink pens that scan fax and email to places.

- Develop a college degree book with degree in back for non essential issues/professions.

- Automated phoneline for coupons to be mailed to your home.

- Start your own paper magazine.

- Sell fold up purses/pocketbooks.

- Self service DVD purchase counter.

- Flameless state/country adventure vanilla or other scented candles.

- Develop sneaker boots or sneakers with socks attached.

- Calendar bags.

- A professional book with certificate at the back for certain professions that are possible to be done in this city. DVD/CD optional i.e. tap dance, etc.

- Start a messenger/delivery service in your area.

- Start your own fashion collection

- Start your own small farm.

- Open your own small grocery store. Be nice, be good.

- Develop your own school.

- Start an actor's/extra association to get movies done on your own or elsewhere.

- Sell prepackaged popcorn.

- Sell baseballs/all around balls.

- Grocery/ restaurant self service use debit cards/cash machines for checkout.

- Sell voice technology printers.

- Make/develop/sell business plans.

- Develop flu patch sold over the counter with no prescription/ doctor, nurse or pharmacist not needed.

- Develop scanner for teeth with printer capability attached or close.

- Make wine scotch liquids.

- Develop DVD same day movie release production service legally/legitimately.

- Develop an automated sales line

- Develop water irrigation systems needed in countries like Africa, etc.

- Develop a car with latch at the bottom to walk with options.

- Try to make/growbell/develop anything imported cheaper thru an undercut, i.e. anything made overseas go to made in U.S.A. or locally.

- Develop alternate sources of energy, communication, power, food, housing.

- Always use a prepaid debit card or small cash when possible.

- Automated newspaper dispenser.

- Make anything legal cheaper, that's safe to manufacture.

- Develop a DVD, CD, book with certificate for a defensive driving course to get credit on licenses for driving in addition to the internet for safe driving as well.

- Start your own school.

- Start a neighborhood consignment/pawnshop.

- Become a cheap car dealer by automated phone, fax, online or in person.

- Develop home cars. Cars that you can live in sometime if possible.

- Develop a lawyer by mail correspondence course if you can get the authorization with diploma at the back or just mail it. (I would be interested, please contact directly at 347-410-7480 if done)

- Develop an optician, doctor or dentist by mail correspondence course with diploma at the back or to be mailed. (I would be interested, please contact directly at 347-410-7480 if done)

- Do a website that prints a family tree individual/person enters data.

- Business plan website, automated phone generation, fax, mail.

- A security police contract.

- Debt clearance company

- Develop an alternative to our current light/gas/cable system besides what we already have. Direct purchase, no billing and affordable.

- Develop a cheap home building company for small homes to be built for land use. Maybe relocated to parks and other sites.

- Become a doctor/dentist or lawyer/doctor.

- Bringing penicillin and steroids over the counter with proper warning labels if possible.

- Set up an account to do money orders.

- Open a 50 cents store for every item.

- Work as many jobs as possible.

- Become a realtor.

- Dried powder soda gingerale, cola, etc.

- Private GED (General high school universal diploma) or develop your own school.

- Do a phone/voice printing system.

- Do a home DNA test kit for genes.

- Do bottled vinegar water/apple vinegar, etc. (helps health and can make money too)

- Develop instant IV pack finger stick with finger holder, if possible.

- Make a wheelchair access/handicap disability small cars.

- Apartment cleaning system.

- Develop a relay phone that prints and reads your voice for over the counter sales.

- Design your own fragrance.

- Develop low on the ground/ floor jeep cars.

- Do a new game for building golf, etc.

- Develop water irrigation systems for dry states like Texas, countries like Africa or do a bottled water brand.

- Develop a scanner that types what is scanned.

- Light steroids sold over the counter. Consumer warning and responsibility disclaimer on product.

- Make stuffed animals/toys.

- Start an online magazine.

- Start an online tax prep program that runs itself

- Sell emergency kits.

- Sell fire extinguishers.

- Sell anything undercut(cheaper)

- Work harder (health provided)

- See if you can offer a cheaper government service.

- Make small cheap battery operated blenders with cup cover.

- Develop 911 call walkie talkies for people. Registered walkie talkies that can radio 911 and talk for emergency personnel or people.

- Lollipop cakes – sticks with small circle cakes on them.

- Develop independent private self serve mailing box outlets with stamps/money orders/ boxes.

- Grocery delivery service (Be good, reliable, reputable and fast in this business)

- Make finger balloons, use gloves.

- Develop CD walkman with radio

- Develop an American taxicab company

- Make finger balloons, use gloves.

STAY ACTIVE

STAY INVOLVED

OBEY THE LAW

START A LITTLE SPORTS TEAM
TO STAY IN SHAPE

BE KIND

THANK YOU

50 Ways
to Make Potatoes

By
Joyce Shearin

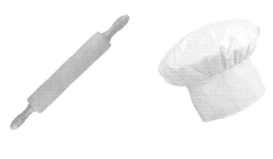

Potato Cake

Make to taste your own
Use Microwave, blender and oven if you desire.

Potato Meal

Make to taste your own
Use Microwave, blender and oven if you desire.

Baked Potatoes with Cheese

Make to taste your own
Use Microwave, blender and oven if you desire.

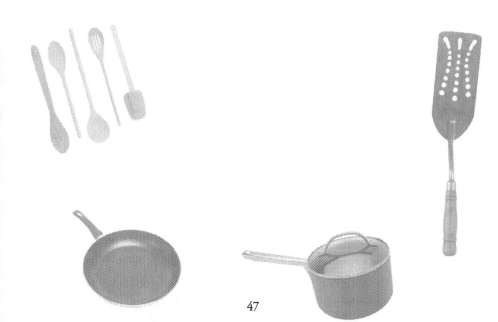

Mashed Potato

Make to taste your own
Use Microwave, blender and oven if you desire.

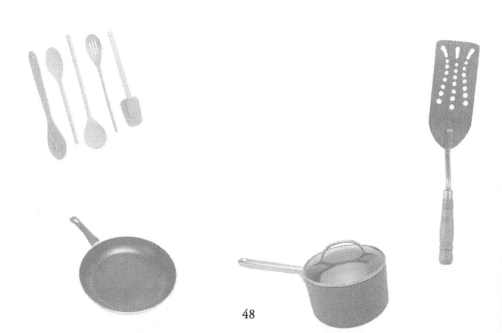

Potato Salad

Make to taste your own
Use Microwave, blender and oven if you desire.

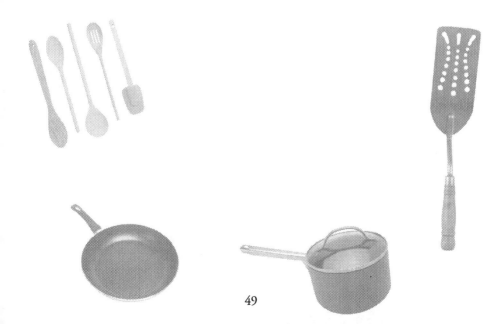

Potato Sandwich

Make to taste your own
Use Microwave, blender and oven if you desire.

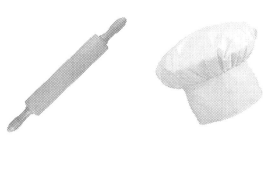

Potato Pie

Make to taste your own
Use Microwave, blender and oven if you desire.

Potato Pizza

Make to taste your own
Use Microwave, blender and oven if you desire.

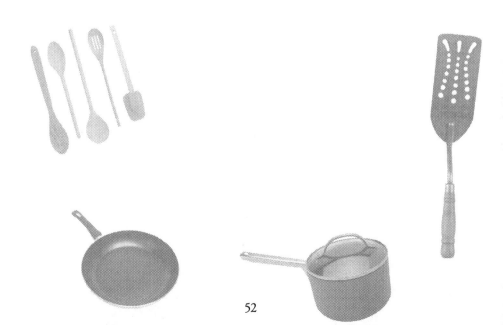

Potato Crepes

Make to taste your own
Use Microwave, blender and oven if you desire.

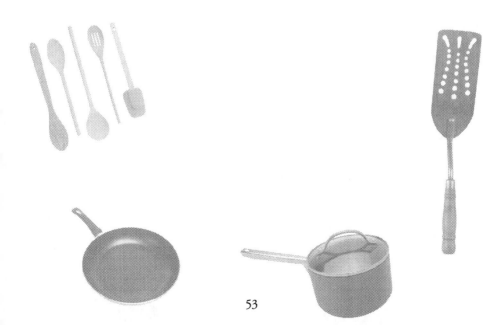

Potato Breakfast Bars

Make to taste your own
Use Microwave, blender and oven if you desire.

Potato Liquid Food

Make to taste your own
Use Microwave, blender and oven if you desire.

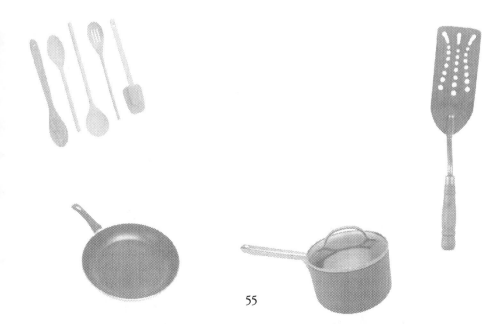

Egg and Potato

Make to taste your own
Use Microwave, blender and oven if you desire.

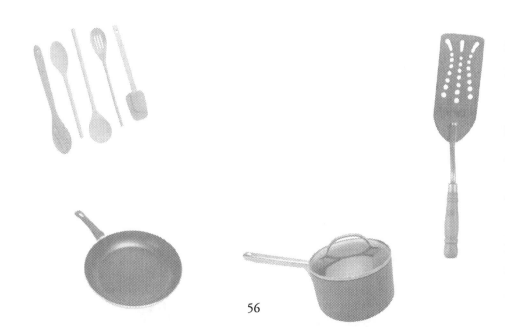

Potato Shells

Make to taste your own
Use Microwave, blender and oven if you desire.

Potato Topping

Make to taste your own
Use Microwave, blender and oven if you desire.

Potato Crepes

Make to taste your own
Use Microwave, blender and oven if you desire.

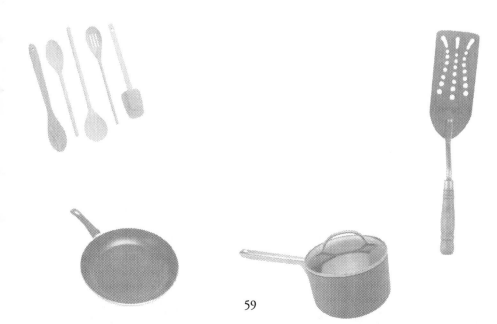

Mashed Potato

Make to taste your own
Use Microwave, blender and oven if you desire.

Potato Pancakes

Make to taste your own
Use Microwave, blender and oven if you desire.

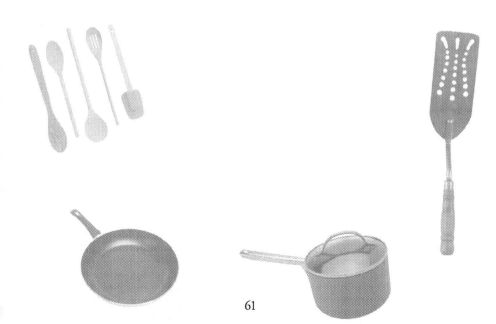

Potato Pancakes

Make to taste your own
Use Microwave, blender and oven if you desire.

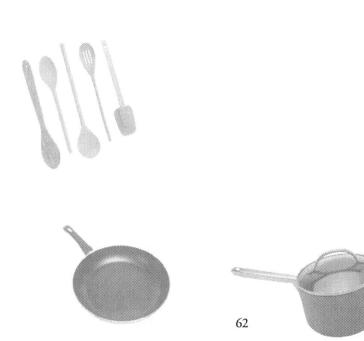

Potato Chips

Make to taste your own
Use Microwave, blender and oven if you desire.

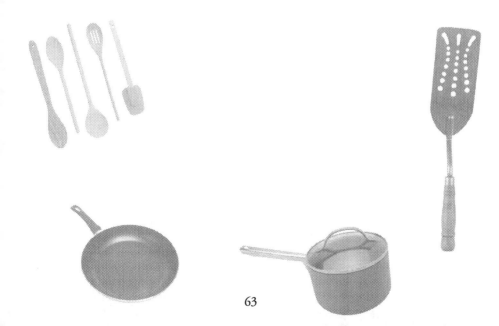

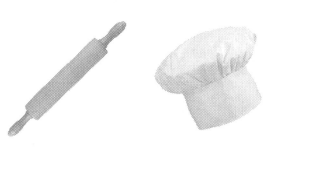

Potato Dips

Make to taste your own
Use Microwave, blender and oven if you desire.

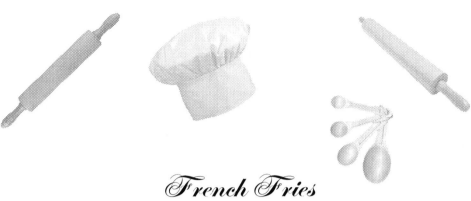

French Fries

Make to taste your own
Use Microwave, blender and oven if you desire.

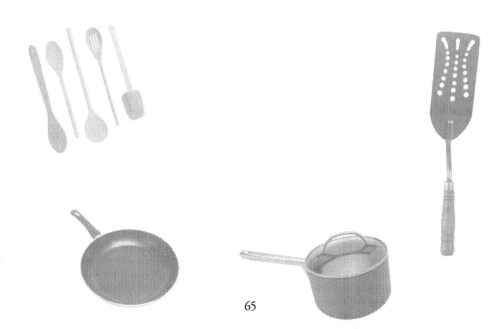

Cooked Potatoes with Skins

Make to taste your own
Use Microwave, blender and oven if you desire.

Boiled Potatoes

Make to taste your own
Use Microwave, blender and oven if you desire.

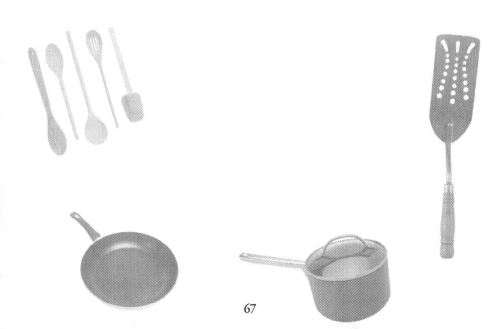

Crispy Potatoes

Make to taste your own
Use Microwave, blender and oven if you desire.

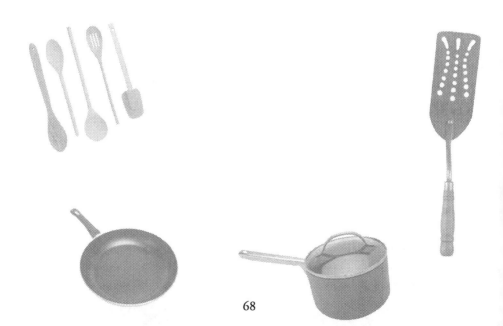

Whipped Potatoes

Make to taste your own
Use Microwave, blender and oven if you desire.

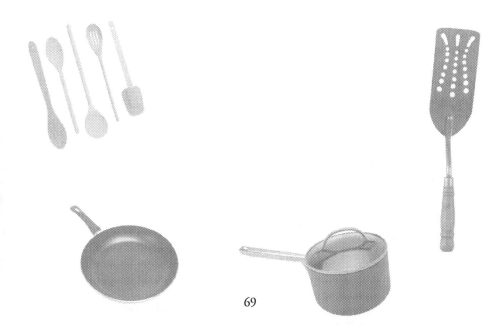

Potato Spread

Make to taste your own
Use Microwave, blender and oven if you desire.

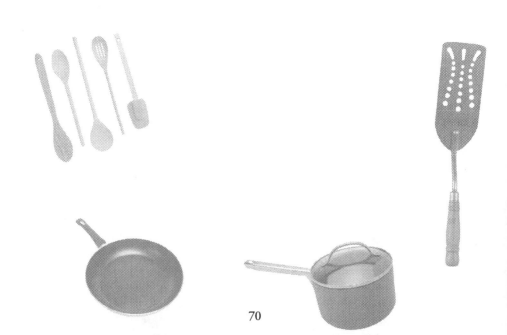

Onion Potato Snacks

Make to taste your own
Use Microwave, blender and oven if you desire.

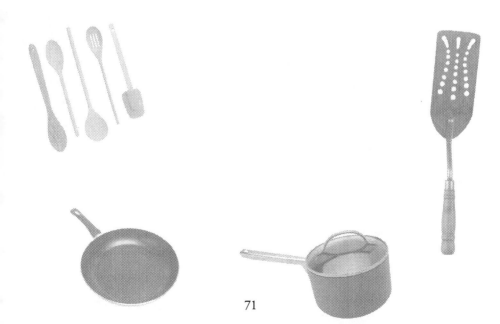

Steamed Potato

Make to taste your own
Use Microwave, blender and oven if you desire.

Potato Biscuit

Make to taste your own
Use Microwave, blender and oven if you desire.

Potato Bread

Make to taste your own
Use Microwave, blender and oven if you desire.

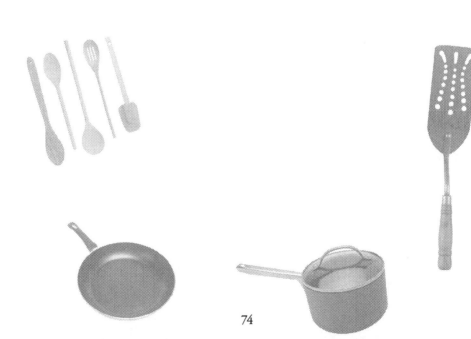

Potato Powder

Make to taste your own
Use Microwave, blender and oven if you desire.

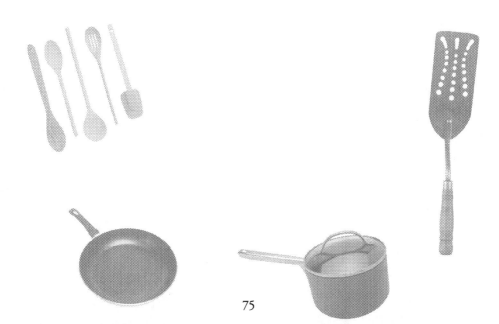

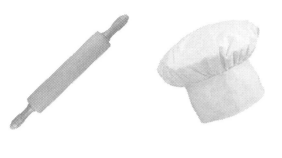

Potato Powder

Make to taste your own
Use Microwave, blender and oven if you desire.

Potato Beans
(use smalls potatoes)

Make to taste your own
Use Microwave, blender and oven if you desire.

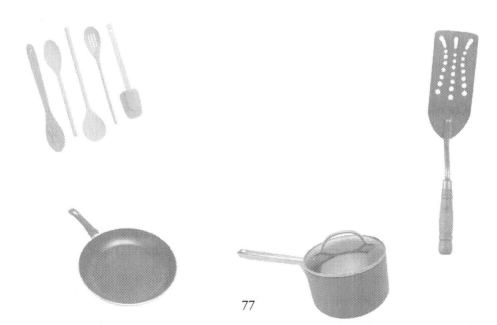

Potato and Peanut Butter

Make to taste your own
Use Microwave, blender and oven if you desire.

Barbeque Potatoes

Make to taste your own
Use Microwave, blender and oven if you desire.

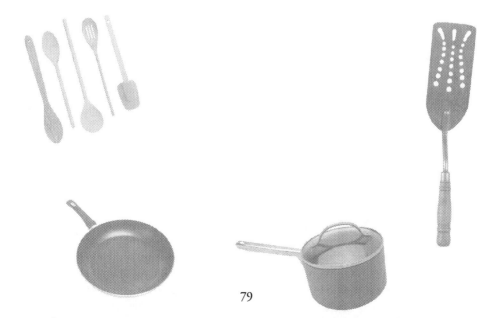

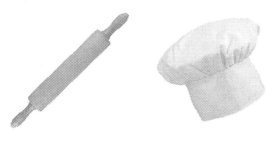

Potato Cookies

Make to taste your own
Use Microwave, blender and oven if you desire.

Creamy Magical Whipped Potatoes

Make to taste your own
Use Microwave, blender and oven if you desire.

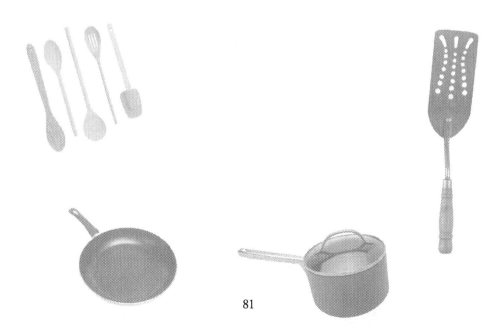

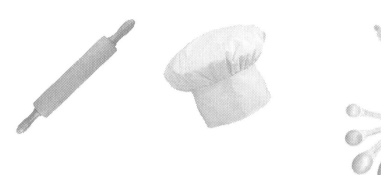

Potato Flakes

Make to taste your own
Use Microwave, blender and oven if you desire.

Potato Seasoning

Make to taste your own
Use Microwave, blender and oven if you desire.

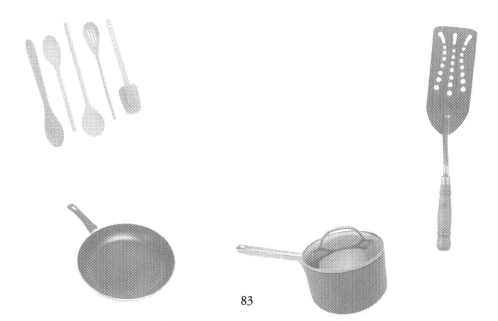

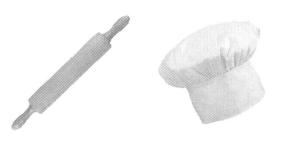

Potato bites

Make to taste your own
Use Microwave, blender and oven if you desire.

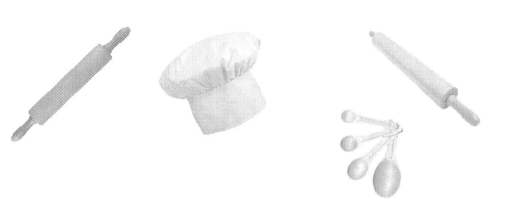

20 Ways to use Corn

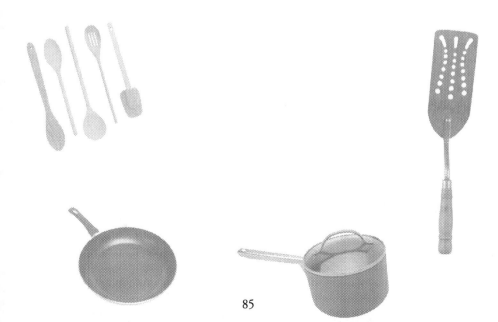

Corn Flour

Make to taste your own
Use Microwave, blender and oven if you desire.

Corn Stew

Corn Dog

Make to taste your own
Use Microwave, blender and oven if you desire.

Cooked Corn

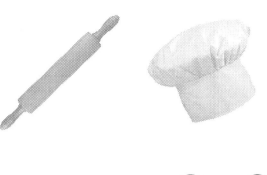

Corn Cake

Make to taste your own
Use Microwave, blender and oven if you desire.

Corn Pie

Corn Cereal

Make to taste your own
Use Microwave, blender and oven if you desire.

Corn Ears

Corn Meal

Make to taste your own
Use Microwave, blender and oven if you desire.

Corn Salad

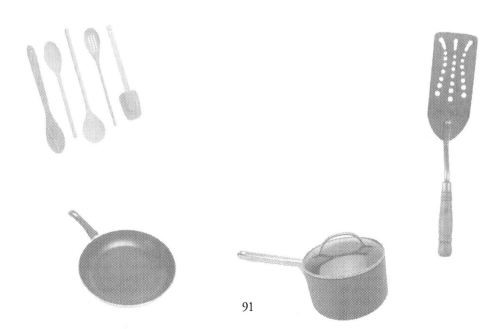

Fried Corn

Make to taste your own
Use Microwave, blender and oven if you desire.

Mashed Corn

Corn and Potato

Make to taste your own
Use Microwave, blender and oven if you desire.

Corn and Rice

Corn Sauce

Make to taste your own
Use Microwave, blender and oven if you desire.

Corn Dough

Tips To Make
Extra Money

1. Convert a hobby

2. Work part-time

3. Volunteer (sometimes they might help back or tip)

4. Become an extra actor or actress

5. Start a small farm

6. Join a union (sometimes it helps)

Thank you

This book is dedicated to the ones I love.